In 2008, when Guernsey started its own Blue Plaque scheme to celebrate its most famous residents, the first plaque was erected in honour of G.B. Edwards, on Hawkesbury, the house in which he had grown up.

In the thirty-five years since the book's publication, Edward Chaney amassed a wealth of information about the author, who had done everything he could to frustrate a biographer. In 2015, Chaney published the results in a biography, *Genius Friend*, which included Edwards's family origins in Guernsey, his early promise as a writer, and how he sank into obscurity as a civil servant during World War 2 until he resurfaced in Weymouth after his retirement.

This guide is based on research into Gerald's family in Guernsey, and shows how events in his own life directly inspired events in his novel. It combines real locations associated with the author and his family, as well as those that feature in the novel.

The trail is laid out in a suggested sequence – but as it balances the fictional with the real life story – the sequence is neither chronological nor in the sequence of the book. It can therefore be followed from cover-to-cover, or used as a guide to make an informed detour along-side other trips. It is by no means exhaustive – for example, it does not attempt to include places in St Peter Port referred to in the novel, which could be the subject of another similar-sized guide.

This guide is also illustrated with relevant quotes from *The Book of Ebenezer*. Should you wish to refer to them in their original context, the page numbers are provide on the NYRB Classics 2007

It should be possible, travell (or bicycle for the more e to cover most of these lo a day. As with any Guerns it is advisable to equip yourself with the latest edition of Perry's Guide map. Grid references are provided to help locate them.

Gerald Edwards (seated) with Clarrie Bellot, c. 1918 (courtesy Edward Chaney)

CHOUET

Les Moulins Ⓐ *Perry's Guide Ref: 6 A2*

We start this tour at Chouet, the fictional location of Les Moulins, the home of Ebenezer Le Page. In his own words:-

> When the quarries opened in the North, and there was good money to be made; and my grandfather, who was no higher than a cook aboard ship, gave up going to sea and worked in the Chouey quarry. He can't have done too bad. It was him built Les Moulins, where I have lived all my life. It is built of solid, blue Guernsey granite and will last forever. It ought to, too. It cost a hundred pounds; and that's a lot of money. (*Ebenezer*, p.7).

All that can now be seen are the Napoleonic defences – a granite loophole tower and magazine. Gerald Edwards deliberately chose the location because he knew that there was no-one living there.

> Le Pages are as common as Smiths over here; but there is no Ebenezer Le Page living at Les Moulins for the simple reason it isn't there, nor can La Petite Grève be found on the map (Letter to Edward Chaney, *Genius Friend*, p.286)

In the 1901 census, there were several families living on this headland – includ-

Photo: Kay Martin

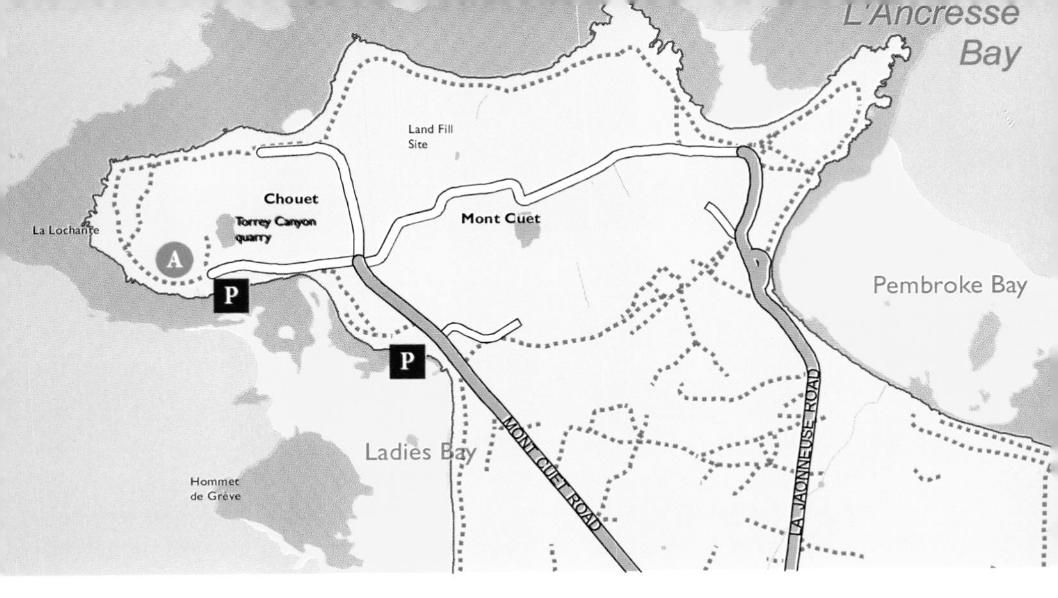

ing one living in the loophole tower. Look for the copse of pine trees opposite the car park. It has been suggested that the derelict granite wall beneath the pines could be the remains of one of the houses that formerly stood here.

The best description of Les Moulins comes from Ebenezer's description of Neville Falla's painting:

> Well, nobody could have any doubt what it was meant to be. It was Les Moulins and no other house; and even more old-fashioned than it is. … The walls got narrower as they went up, and the chimney stacks smaller; but the windows shone brightly in the sun. The wallflowers in front was really beautiful; and there was the old grey wall of the garden, and the white gate, and the green front door. The apple-tree at the side was skew-jiffy, and the windmill was peeping over the roof. (*Ebenezer*, p.365).

Today, this part of the island is best known for Mont Cuet landfill site. This disused quarry is nearly full. Ebenezer's Chouet quarry probably refers to what is now know as Torrey Canyon quarry, as this was where the oil recovered from the sea was deposited following the major 1970s oil spill.

Parking: There is a small car park near the loophole tower. There is also ample parking at the northern end of Ladies' Bay – from where you can follow the footpath to the loophole tower.

OATLANDS

Oatlands Village (B) *Perry's ref: 10 B2*

Our next stop is Oatlands Village, which is the best place to park to see Hawkesbury, the house where Gerald Edwards grew up. But it does have its own part in Ebenezer's story.

This farmhouse was once the home of Philemon Fleure Dorey, who, along with his brothers John and Arthur, was one of the founders of Fruit Export, which they established in 1904 to market and export Guernsey horticultural produce in England. During most of the 20th century, tomato exports were the island's main industry, employing almost 50% of the population.

Although the island tomato industry is no more – the last exports were sent to England in 2013 – Fruit Export is still in existence. Now known as Blue Diamond, it owns a chain of garden centres.

Ebenezer's mother used to pickle her ormers in vinegar, and bay leaves from Mr Dorey's garden:

> We didn't have no bay leaves in our garden; so I had to go and steal some from Mr Dorey of Oatlands. He had a bay tree with leaves hanging over the road. Mr Dorey would have given us as many bay leaves as we wanted, if we'd asked him; but my mother wouldn't let me. She was proud, my mother. She would rather steal than beg. (*Ebenezer*, p.16)

Ebenezer also worked at the vinery of a Mr Dorey – but this is believed to have been inspired by Philemon's brother Arthur, who owned Belgrave Vinery at the Halfway.

> My father said to my mother, 'Our boy is not going to work in the quarries.' 'What then?' said my mother. 'We must find something better for him to do than that,' he said. I don't know if it was better, I don't think it was; but when I left school he got me a job in Dorey's Vineries. They was still growing grapes, but trying out tomatoes under the vines … It turned out there was a better sale in England for the tomatoes and in the end the greenhouses grew nothing else. (*Ebenezer*, p.14)

Hawkesbury (C)

Perry's ref: 10 B2

Gerald Edwards was born in 1899 at Sous Les Hougues (see p.13). The following year, his parents, Tom Edwards and his second wife Harriet *née* Mauger bought a plot on the Oatlands Estate from P.F. Dorey on which they built Hawkesbury.

Tom, Harriet and Gerald can be found living here in the 1901 and 1911 census with Gerald's half-sister, Kathleen, Tom's daughter from his first marriage. Gerald left the island in 1917, initially with the army to Southampton, and from there to Bristol University to study English Literature. He never lived in Guernsey again, although visited his family occasionally.

Photo: Edward Chaney

His mother Harriet died in 1924, and three years later Tom remarried and bought a new property, Les Rosiers, with his new wife. Tom sold Hawkesbury two years later, thereby disinheriting Gerald – in the same way as Harold Martel sold his home to disinherit his son Raymond.

In 2008, Guernsey's first Blue Plaque was erected on Hawkesbury to mark G.B. Edwards's childhood home.

Braeside (D) *Perry's ref: 10 A2*

On the way back to Oatlands Village you will pass Braeside. This old Guernsey house stands at the cross-roads used to identify where the Martel brothers built the houses Wallabaloo and Timbuctoo for their wives, Ebenezer's aunts, Hetty and Prissy.

> 'Well, if she's going to call hers Wallaballoo, I'm going to call ours Timbuctoo!' She did, too. There they are to this day, the two houses, in the meadow the other side of Braye-side with a high wall between them. (*Ebenezer*, p.24)

But again these sisters' houses are fictitious:

> The houses of the Martel brothers could not have existed where they are placed, for it was an open green meadow until well after the end of the First World War. (G.B. Edwards, Letter to Edward Chaney, *Genius Friend*, p.286)

From Oatlands Village, turn left into Les Gigands, and turn right into Les Effards.

Les Gigands (E) *Perry's ref: 10 B3*

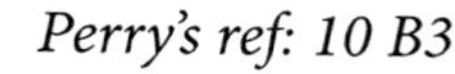

Another old Guernsey farmhouse which is the supposed home of Ebenezer's best friend, Jim Mahy.

> It's true Jim's people was much better off than us; but they never made me feel it. I was always made welcome. His father owned the farm and the cottages and vergees of land; though most of it has long since been sold, and there are bungalows built where Jim and me used to cross the meadows to stake the cows. The farm itself is a guest-house now and owned by I don't know who … The kitchen where I ate so many meals with him was three or four times the size of ours; and there was lovely copper pots and pans on the walls, and always a big fire blazing on the hearth (*Ebenezer*, p.39).

Unfortunately, there is not much of the house to be seen from the road, and there is nowhere convenient to park.

Les Rosiers, Les Effards 

Perry's ref: 10 A3

Photo: Ciprian Ilie

Gerald's father, Tom Edwards, bought this house and adjacent vinery with his third wife, Rosina. The house can be seen, although the site of the vinery on the opposite side of the road has been redeveloped into houses, now called Clos des Rosiers.

Gerald related how his father was reluctant to give up his work in the stone trade:-

> I was only truly in touch with him on one occasion; and that was in 1938, the year of the Munich Crisis, when I visited him at Les Rosiers, where he ran a small growing concern, the quarry having been worked out. He was rather humiliated, though over 80, by being reduced to so effete an occupation. He regarded quarrying granite as the only work fit for a man (*Genius Friend*, p.245).

Tom Edwards's marriage to Rosina Cooke had direct parallels with Raymond's father, Harold, who married his housekeeper, Mrs. Crewe, when Raymond's mother, Hetty, died.

> After the Liberation, Mrs Crewe kept on being as mingy as before with the food; and wouldn't let Harold buy any new clothes. 'It is his grave clothes he must be thinking about now,' she said. He wasn't allowed to get out of his bed, except to do his business in a commode. He had nothing to wear. I don't think he had anything to wear in bed either. He died that winter. My Cousin Mary Ann said there was nothing to bury him in, but Mrs Crewe's niece was married to Phil Randall, who used to play for the Rangers, and he still had an old football shirt; so Harold was put in his coffin in that. Harold would have turned over in his grave if he had known he was buried in a red and white football shirt. He was all for the North. (*Ebenezer*, p.298)

When Tom Edwards died in 1946, Rosina had him buried in the Foulon Cemetery in the same plot where she had buried her first husband. We have been unable to establish what he was wearing.

Parking: St Sampson's High School.

HAUTE CAPELLES

Haute Capelles School *Perry's ref: 9 G3*

Gerald initially attended the Misses Cohu's School (Albion Terrace, Halfway) and then went to Haute Capelles Primary School, from where he gained a scholarship to the States Intermediate School (now the Grammar School).

He returned to Haute Capelles as a pupil-teacher in about 1914 – but his mother arranged for him to be transferred to Vauvert (in St Peter Port) because he had fallen in love with Miss Christine Waymouth, whose father ran the bakery at L'Islet and Harriet did not approve of her. Miss Waymouth, who was born in the same year as Gerald (1899), continued to teach at Haute Capelles school until the late 1950s.

It seems more than a coincidence that Raymond fell for a pupil-teacher called Christine that his mother did not approve of Christine Mahy was the cousin of Ebenezer's best friend, Jim Mahy. Ebenezer did not have a very good opinion of her either:

> I put Christine down as one of those who looked like she was cool, but was hot. I had seen her out with the Renouf brothers and the Birds from St Sampsons; and they wasn't at all the sort of boys who would go out with the Virgin Mary. She was a pupil-teacher in St Sampson's Infants' School; and it was not long after I had seen her talking to Raymond that she went away to England to study for two years in a Training College.
>
> When I saw Raymond again I mentioned that I had seen him talking to Christine. 'For goodness sake, don't tell my mother!' he said. 'What d'you take me for?' I said. 'It's only platonic,' he said, 'we were talking about Robert Browning.' 'Who's he?' I said. 'A poet,' he said... I didn't think Hetty had much to fear from Christine Mahy. (*Ebenezer*, pp.55-6)

THE BRIDGE, ST SAMPSON'S

St Sampson's Harbour (G) *Perry's ref: 11 F3*

St Sampson's harbour grew up during the 19th century as a result of the stone trade. The majority of the island's quarries were in the north, and the stone merchants had their main offices around the harbour, from where they shipped their granite to England. From the mid 19th century until the 1920s, it was also home to six shipbuilding yards.

Many of the businesses and shops mentioned in *Ebenezer* would have been familiar sights here, including: Bird's Coal yard, Mowlem's stone-cracking yard, Tozer's newsagent, Stonelake the Chemist and Leale's hardware store.

Ebenezer talked fondly about how he used to come down to the harbour with his father:

> … then he would take me down to St Sampson's to see the ships. St Sampson's Harbour was full of sailing ships in those days, and there would be three or four anchored in the Roads outside waiting to come in. I couldn't make up my mind if I wanted to work down the quarry, or go to sea when I grew up; but sail was fast giving way to steam, and when it was nearly all steam-boats in St Sampson's Harbour I didn't have the same feeling for going to sea. (p.5)

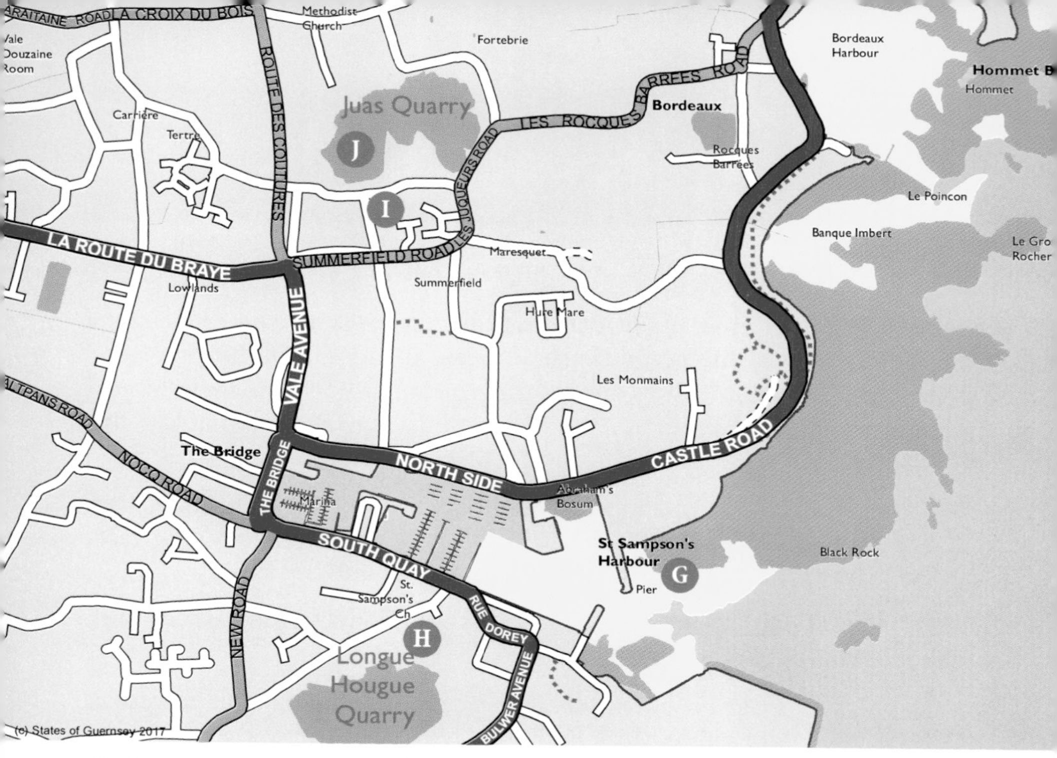

St Sampson's Church H *Perry's ref: 11 F3*

St Sampson's Church is one of the island's ten parish churches and is said to be the oldest in the island – founded in the year 1111. It is named after Samson of Dol, a Welshman who arrived in Guernsey from Brittany in the sixth century introducing Christianity to the island, and became the island's patron saint.

Brothers Harold and Percy Martel married Ebenezer's aunts, Hetty and Prissy, here:-

> The Martels of Ronceval was Church and the two brothers married at St Sampson's Church on the same day and went on the same boat to England and in the same train to London for their honeymoon. (*Ebenezer*, p.24)

Sous Les Hougues  *Perry's ref: 11 F2*

This fine old Guernsey granite house was where Gerald Edwards was born. His parents lived here in the 1890s, before moving to Hawkesbury.

Gerald's account, as with much of his family history, is somewhat romanticised:

> My grandfather … migrated to Guernsey at the age of 19 for the 'stone-rush', when the quarries of the north were opened. It was a hard life. My father

> … sailed and 'saw the world' until he came home and married at the age of 26. He wouldn't have come home then, except that he never overcame his tendency to sea-sickness. He worked for his father, who was by now a quarry-owner, and in due course inherited the quarry and the house, Sous les Hougues, where I was born. (Letter to Edward Chaney, *Genius Friend*, pp. 17-18)

Juas Quarry  *Perry's ref: 11 F1*

Sous Les Hougues is adjacent to Juas Quarry, one of the largest in the island. Now used by the States Water Board for water storage – they acquired three adjacent disused quarries in 1933 and blasted them into one.

The largest of the three quarries was operated by John Mowlem. One of the smaller ones, known as 'Queen's Quarry', was operated by A&F Manuelle, and their initials can be seen carved into the granite gate posts.

Like Gerald's father Tom, Ebenezer's father also worked in a quarry. Ebenezer's boss appears to be a fictional version of Gerald's father (Mauger was Gerald's mother's maiden name):

> He worked for old Tom Mauger from Sous Les Hougues in the Queen's quarry from seven in the morning to six at night, and took his dinner with him in a tin, and a can of tea he kept warm by the stove in the toolhouse. (*Ebenezer*, p4)

Photo: Ciprian Ilie

BORDEAUX

Bordeaux Harbour  *Perry's ref: 11 H1*

This harbour was originally built for fishing boats, but when the island's stone trade developed, it was used to load ships with stone from the nearby Bordeaux quarry. Guernsey merchants were involved in trade with Bordeaux over the centuries, and it is believed that the area derived its name from trading links with that medieval French port.

Ebenezer mentions Bordeaux Harbour in his book – but spells it Birdo – which is how he would have pronounced it. When Neville Falla brings some of his paintings around to show him, Ebenezer writes:

> There was one of Birdo Harbour at low tide, and Herm quite close. It was evening and shining peaceful with a few boats on the quiet sea. He thought it was the best he had done so far, and I thought it was good; but the one I liked best myself was on L'Ancresse Common (p.365).

Bordeaux Quarry  *Perry's ref: 11 H1*

Bordeaux quarry was where Gerald's father, Tom, worked. Tom's father, George, owned land nearby. The photograph below shows Tom Edwards in Bordeaux quarry with his men.

Photo: Edward Chaney

Bordeaux Quarry was used as the island's main landfill site during the 1970s and early 80s. Once it was full, the site was reclaimed as a nature reserve, where there is ample car parking.

Bordeaux Methodist Chapel, Les Grippios (M) *Perry's ref: 11 G1*

This chapel appears in Ebenezer as Birdo Mission Hall and is where Raymond preached his one and only sermon in Guernsey, before he got the sack for his controversial views on religion. See *Ebenezer*, Chapter 8, page 173 onwards.

Photo: Visit Guernsey

LANDES DU MARCHÉ

Mauger family - back row (left to right): Mary Ann, Louisa, Daniel senior, Charlotte junior; front row: Rachel, Daniel junior, Harriet, Charlotte senior.

Le Petit Desert N *(Perry: 9 E5)*

This old Guernsey cottage, Le Petit Désert, is opposite Landes du Marché garage. This was the home of Gerald's mother's family. Her parents, Daniel and Charlotte Mauger, moved into the house in the 1850s, and had a family of 3 sons and 5 daughters. The eldest daughter, Charlotte Mauger married Nicolas Le Page, and her two youngest sisters married two brothers. Harriet, Gerald's mother married Tom Edwards and Rachel married his brother George. This directly inspired the three Le Page sisters: Charlotte, Ebenezer's mother, and her younger sisters Harriet and Priscille who married brothers Harold and Percy Martel.

According to Gerald's letters, his cousin Edwin Le Page was still living in this house in the 1960s.

Photo: Stephen Foote

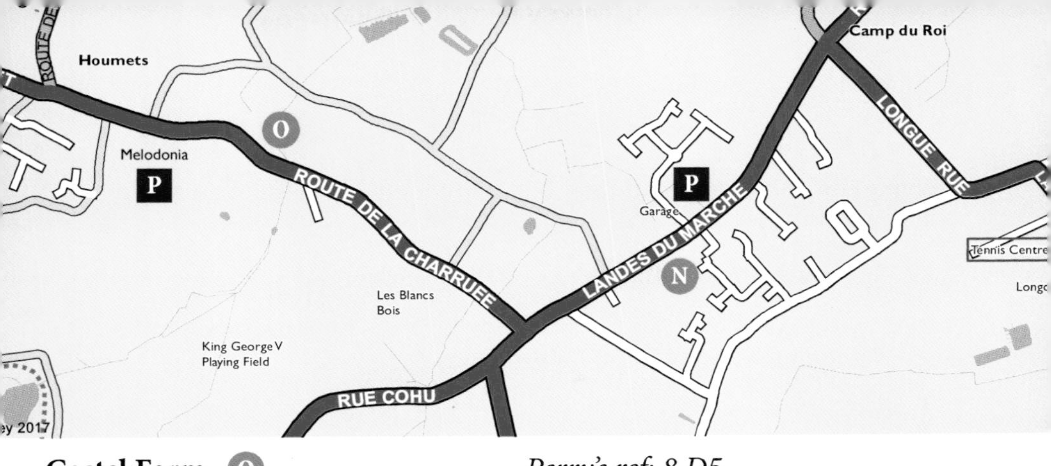

Castel Farm 

Perry's ref: 8 D5

Parking: Melodonia, Rue des Charruées (caution: this is a narrow, winding, busy road with no footpath – so please take care).

The house now called Charruée Lodge was once called Castel Farm, when Gerald's grandfather, George, bought it in 1884. When his wife died, he remarried and moved to Alderney – selling the farm to his son, George.

George junior and his family lived here with his younger brother William. William committed suicide – in the same way as Ebenezer's Uncle Willie does (and perhaps for the same reasons):

> He didn't manage his own affairs very well, my uncle Willie... The evening before the wedding he said he was going to shoot rabbits on Jerbourg. When long after dark he didn't come back, young de Lisle went to look for him and found him shot dead through the head. (*Ebenezer*, p.6)

George and Rachel had three children – Archibald, Horace (who died aged 5 yrs, like Cyril Martel in *Ebenezer*), and Herbert.

Archie Edwards got a girl pregnant and she was sent to stay with his grandmother in Alderney to have the baby, whilst Archie was sent to America. This directly inspired the events in *Ebenezer* with Horace Martel and Isobel Mansell.

> He put Isobel Mansell in the family way and Percy said if that was all he could do, the only place for him was America. (*Ebenezer*, p.50)

Rachel died before the occupation, but George and Herbert lived at Castel Farm throughout the war. Herbert died shortly afterwards from the effects of malnutrition. George sold the farm, and moved to St Peter Port, where he died in 1949.

GRAND HAVRE & L'ISLET

Vale Church (P) *Perry's ref: 6 B5*

Directly across the bay from Chouet is the nearest church to Les Moulins. It is also the church in which Gerald Edwards was baptised.

> I have lived all my days to the sound of bells of the Vale Church, coming to me on the wind over the water. When I was a boy I used to hear them playing a hymn of a Sunday evening, and then the quick ding-dong, ding-dong, before the service began; and I would hear them practising of a Wednesday night… (*Ebenezer*, p.57)

Grand Havre Regatta  *Perry's ref: 6 A5*

This bay is the site of the regatta in which young Ebenezer won the leg of mutton by scaling a greasy pole, and earns himself the nickname Monkey Le Page. Nearing the end of his life, he reminisces to the young artist, Neville Falla about what he considers his greatest achievement:

> When we got to the Grand Havre, it was dull and grey … yet it was alive with gay marquees and boats sailing, and the sun was shining, and all the boys I knew was there: and I could hear their thick Guernsey voices shouting 'Bien fait, Monkey! Bien fait, Monkey Le Page!' and Jim was nursing the leg of mutton as if it was a bunch of flowers, and everybody laughing. I don't know how I looked, but Neville said 'What you thinking now, Funny-face?' as if I was a child. I didn't want to brag; yet I wanted him to know I had done something once. I said 'They used to have the Regatta on Grand Havre, and one year I won the leg of mutton off the greasy pole.' (*Ebenezer*, p. 392)

L'Islet Cromlech  *Perry's ref: 10 A1*

The discovery of this prehistoric monument in 1912 provoked headlines in local newspapers. Ebenezer relates the story to visiting archaeologist Dudley Waine which leads to the 'discovery' of a similar site behind Les Moulins.

> Also, a few years before the War they uncovered some stones at L'Islet was supposed to be a prehistorical burial ground or something; but anybody could have arranged those. I was saying all this to try my best to be helpful, when all of a sudden he clapped his hands to his brow as it he had seen a vision, and was staring through his spectacles at the stones on the top of my

wall. 'It is not possible!' he said, 'Where have those come from?' I said the builder got them out of the gully: I didn't think to say Percy had chipped pieces off to make them look ornamental. Dudley Waine was down the gully like a dog after a rabbit … Those stones on top of my wall was prehistorical axe-heads. (*Ebenezer*, p.163)

Postcard, Thomas Bramley, c.1912 (courtesy Michael Deane)

ROCQUAINE & PLEINMONT

Rocquaine Bay is at the south-west corner of the island, just about as far from Les Moulins as it is possible to get in Guernsey.

Liza Queripel's house  *Perry's ref: 26 A2*

Although it is not clear exactly where Liza lived, we know it was near the Imperial Hotel, the landmark pub which overlooks the bay.

> I got off the bus at the Imperial and walked back along the grass. The old house was still there and had the same crooked chimney and the wicked windows that looked at you sideways from under the thatch. (*Ebenezer*, p.203)

Fort Grey *(26 B1)* 

Looking out across the bay, you can see the Napoleonic fortification, Fort Grey.This is where Ebenezer and Jim came to the Fête for the Coronation of King George V. Liza was in the parade dressed as Britannia. After the parade Ebenezer took her for a romantic walk across the beach.

> She gave me her hand to help her down over the rocks as we walked across Rocquaine Bay towards Fort Grey. She asked me if I knew the story of how it was Fort Grey came to be haunted. I didn't. She said that hundreds of years ago, when it was Rocqaine Castle, two young lovers sat on the wall in each other's arms by moonlight and threw themselves into the sea. 'Whatever did they want to do that for?' I said. 'They was lovers,' she said. 'They was mad,' I said. (*Ebenezer*, pp.73-4)

This started a row, which ended with Ebenezer pushing Liza and her falling into a rock pool.

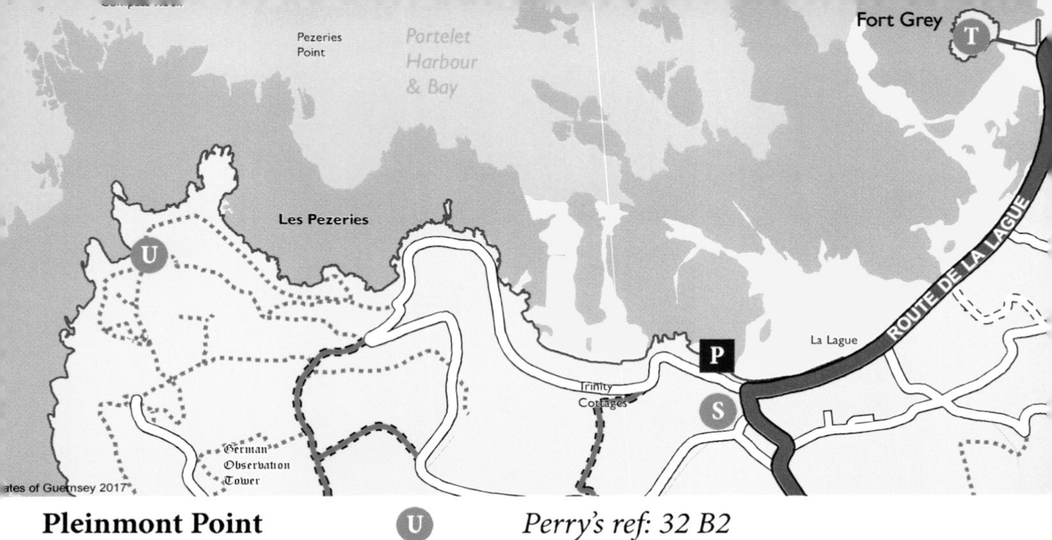

Pleinmont Point

U *Perry's ref: 32 B2*

Where Horace and Raymond met their untimely ends during the German Occupation. After his breakdown, Raymond was staying with Liza. In spite of everything that had happened, when Horace appeared at the door, Raymond was thrilled to see his cousin again:

> 'Let's go as far as the two big rocks!', he said to Raymond, 'I want to see the Hanois light.' 'It isn't lit!' she screamed at them. Horace flung the door open, and stood with his fist up, the big fool. 'It will be lit again!' (*Ebenezer*, p.260)

When they fail to return, Liza asks her German officer friend if he had heard anything. He said a mine had exploded between the two big rocks that night.

> There was no saying what caused it. If Raymond and Horace had happened to have touched the fuse by standing on it, they would have been blown to pieces in the sea. There was blood on the stones below.

Park at Rocquaine Bay and follow the path along to the *Table des Pions* (Fairy Ring), where the two big rocks can be clearly seen. As you approach the gap between the rocks, the Hanois Lighthouse can be seen out at sea.

Left: Fort Grey
Right: 'the two big rocks' at Pleinmont
(Photos: Kay Martin)

LIHOU ISLAND

Photo: Visit Guernsey

Lihou island (*Perry's ref: 12 C2*) is a small tidal island just off Guernsey's west coast. From the twelfth century until 1560, it was the home to a Benedictine Priory, under the control of Mont St Michel. The ruins of the priory can still be seen. It can be accessed on foot by an ancient stone causeway at low tide – but the tide can come in very quickly, and it is easy to get caught out (do check tides before you go).

Ebenezer and Jim visit Lihou as part of a day out cycling around the island. They forget the time, and are stranded overnight.

> By the time we got back to the L'Erée end again, the sea was over the causeway. He couldn't swim and nor could I, and to get back up to our waists in the water it was hopeless to try because the current is very strong there, and we would have only been swept out to sea. Jim said, 'Well it looks as if this is going to be our home for the night.' (*Ebenezer*, p.45).

The ensuing scene has prompted a debate as to the nature of the relationship between Ebenezer and Jim. Recent discoveries about Edwards's lifestyle would suggest that he intended their relationship to be closer than mere friendship.

GRANDES ROCQUES

In the final chapter, Neville takes Ebenezer for a ride in his car. They go down to Rocquaine, where they visit Liza Queripel, and, even though Ebenezer has not seen her for years, they find her at home in her cottage at Rocquaine.

On the way home, Neville drives Ebenezer back along the west coast back to Les Moulins. As Ebenezer's story nears its end, he and Neville stop to witness an incredible sunset at Grandes Rocques (*Perry's ref: 8 A2*):

> The sun was going down and clouds coming from nowhere, so it seemed, as if they was hurrying for a great event. There was heavy clouds low down, and high mountains of clouds, and fluffy clouds loose in the air, and others like feathers overhead; and all the way round Vazon they was changing from white and grey to red and gold. At Albecq, the rocks was red; and from Cobo, the sun was a huge ball of fire, floating in a cave of fire, and half under the sea. I couldn't bear it. I was going to shout to Neville 'Stop, stop please: you are killing me!' when at Gran'-Rock he drew in to the side of the road of his own accord and switched the engine off. 'This is too good to miss,' he said: and we sat and watched the big sun sink lower and lower, until there was only a tip showing: when suddenly, it dipped under, and was gone!
>
> 'God, that's magnificent!', said Neville. I had no words but Raymond's. 'It is a glimpse of the world as God made it,' I said, 'on the first evening of the first day.' He gave me a funny look. 'I'd love to paint it!' he said. 'It can never be painted,' I said. (*Ebenezer*, pp. 391-2).

Photo: Jane Mosse

G.B. Edwards and his wife, Kathleen, circa 1926.

ACKNOWLEDGEMENTS

I am most grateful to Professor Edward Chaney, the literary heir of G.B. Edwards, for his permission to include quotes from *The Book of Ebenezer Le Page*, as well as from *Genius Friend*, his biography of G.B. Edwards.

I would also like to thank Jane Mosse and Susan Ilie for their help with the research behind this booklet; Edward Chaney and Sarah Inman for their encouragement; Kay Martin, Jane Mosse, Ciprian Ilie, Michael Deane and Visit Guernsey for photos & Digimap for excerpts from Perry's Guide map.

COPYRIGHT

Published by Blue Ormer Publishing (www.blueormer.co.uk).

Printed in Guernsey by Printed (www.printed.gg).

FURTHER READING

The Book of Ebenezer Le Page by G.B. Edwards is published by NYRB Classics (ISBN: 978-1590172339).

Genius Friend: G.B. Edwards and The Book of Ebenezer Le Page by Edward Chaney is published by Blue Ormer (ISBN: 978-0992879105).

Price £3.99